# toasting to freckles

## Ally Rowe

BookLeaf
Publishing

India | USA | UK

Presentation by *BookLeaf Publishing*

Web: www.bookleafpub.com

E-mail: info@bookleafpub.com


ISBN: 978-93-5744-488-0

First edition 2022

# freckles

//

are the freckles you now bear,
a mark of sun and summer dare?
the reprimand of a blistered ear,
darker speckles coming clear.

or do they come another way,
blown along on a windy day?
fixed upon a slender nose,
gaining numbers as you grow.

perhaps these spots aren't gained at all,
simply hidden when you're small?
outer layers wearing thin,
to reveal what lies beneath your skin.

//

# little rock

//

little rock, she'll likely be,
in their reforming family,
a shock of nordic wispy hair,
with dimpled cheeks; milk soft and fair,
not unlike her newfound brother,
whose tender welcome was like no other,
no 'us and her' or other-ness passed through,
his lips or mind when she came new.
side-by-side, you wouldn't know,
of those eight months and nine below,
distanced by suburb and the world,
'hold tight to mum's finger, little rock,
our girl'.

//

# nocturnal

*//*

rising of that blinding moon,
it's kiss upon young skin,
be up, the night is early still
our secrets to begin.

*//*

# Wilson

//

Wilson writes as he bites down,
and chews on daily news,
over telegrams splayed beside his Muse,
domesticated,
self created,
self berated language used,
one views the day through certain hues,
through cut botanical garden dews,
can-can girls and sweet perfumes,
dated typeface,
faux pas' of gender causes disgrace,
mulled over whilst he eats
thick toast.

//

# washing dishes

//

democracy manifesting
in a lost comfort,
tiptoeing around for the greater good,
in softshoe shuffles,
shifting eyes whilst washing dishes,
speak aloud when I am cold and
need someone to hold.

//

# the jewel box

*//*

a pearl-sized boy, kind and wise,
lay down one evening and closed his eyelids to
the world;
it had been a long day.
high above,
pinpricks of light began to emerge,
in the velveteen canopy,
in which he resided;
the jewel box.
rounded edges met as columns,
in sparkling clusters,
he nestled deeper,
delft blue doona
cocooned his satin shoulders
and back,
one hundred bulbs encrusted above.

*//*

# wild wrought waif

//

tassel, tied,
'not a hassle', died.
and never return to the old tides.

I'd find new ones to bide my time.
thick tanned hide of a homegrown heifer,
restrained by studded ancestral guides,
raging blisters mark the skin,
hung like bunting, I'd like to think,
we took our hooves and sank in
ancient cyclical sands of time.

mussels kiss from shoreline dusk,
and serve as shark bait with coconut husks,
shared with the cow and the wild wrought waif,
set on bony hips.
they'd left her be, essentially.
a rogue irregularity,
a late arrival and always been,
tying up knots, slicing skin,
mending bone and that within,
and now for good and self she'd sewn,
a dozen kelp flasks and shades above,
her own, tide-side abode.

//

# sapphire bike

//

the new bike shone like sapphire,
the tyre, wrapped around its wires,
a long-awaited present,
to admire, fill desire,

to ride one day in many years,
when fewer fears were prying near,
he'd study and pretend gears,
hidden from all eyes and peers.

for that way, no bruise
could prove he could lose,
for no-one was allowed to see him
scrape his knee and ooze.

and before long, the rust clung to every corner of
that sapphire husk,
until that desired gust of wind,
would blow away his dust.

//

# janglin' keys



it only begins when the sensor light quits,
it's a wary beam,
surveying for danger,
knows it's time to leave.
that's when walls come down,
arms unfold and keys are a-janglin'.
freckles blur under night vision,
kindness and intention stir like nocturnal
creatures,
like mice, soft with twitching whiskers and
intuition.

at first, these janglin' keys are big ben;
a formal handshake and bow goodbye as the
moon rises up into the air.
a push from one segment to the next.
but,
nobody really wants to leave,
not after the show for there is so much to say,
so much looking and laughter,
tea and cakes that look so delicious

but I don't dare touch it because it's 10pm and I
really must be going, with all the important
things that the next moment has in store.

then,
the smallest phrase uttered, a question
pauses my inclination to the rusted car door.
a wedge in the door that will only take one
moment.
I reply, short and kind. I present a query,
despite a great BONG BONG of the clock tower
thumping within.
the moon surveys, carrying discourse with her
creamy rays and
the knell fades into her velvet bosom.
such clanging of alarm bells softens to a
wind-chime.
a fae twinkling, light and comforting.
of safety nearby, a lifejacket's whistle breathing
out in a gust of wind.
gentle and true words fill both,
adjusting to the light slowly as she warms us up.
coaxed by the soft janglin'
of my keys and hers.

//

# jinx

//

jinx.
double jinx,
bounce back
as ringlets in sync,
curled helixes slacken
around one another
in soft, cinnamon swirls.
halve your snack
you two,
counting honeyed crumbs,
one for me and one for you.

//

# jacaranda canopies

//

this fine mourning is breaking the hold,
of primitive patterns, of age-old grout,
which grip it's mossy tendrils to mold
each line of speech and what I'm told.

so overdue to pressure-hose
the ingrained grit of lichen foes.
go now,
find your home in the cold pipes so,

the overcast sky and violet can say,
'November's here, spring clean away
the grime of an ally yesterday,
hold out hands to make bold folds
and pray.'

//

# sister



unwarranted indigestion,
seals my throat upon the station,
tell me now,
was there a need to swallow it down
whole and without salivation?
not at all.
the sister who sprinkled her heart and love onto
you waits,
as you race without patience,
her ancient signs for adoration,
my throat choked and I fell late.
a 100s and 1000s moment that sticks,
a kiss on both cheeks for the chef de cuisine,
all will know of her wondrous creations,
of sweet salvation with pink, white and brown,
a glow from a frown,
that familiar groan fades down.
days again, we talk at the station,
my voice filled up with sprinkles of affirmation.

//

# the traveler's game

//

afar;
each day brims with tickets and guides,
pencil sketches of ancient skies,
of foreign notes and vibrant lives,
atlas close and deeper nights...

near;
a weary commuter, trained and tame,
knows nothing of the city's fame,
each day offers the very same
of maps and wonder - the traveler's game.

//

# capture me



an ancient ochre haze cast a strange afternoon
light over us yesterday,
after the fires not far away from home.
planned in advance, routine back-burning, they assured
and I quietly thanked them for setting this scene;

the delicate veil formed and shifted,
descending from sepia eucalypt trees above,
to settle around my crown of ash-speckled hair.
it cast itself about the dry skin of my elbows in
the gentlest, soft gray-blue mirage.
i couldn't help but take
a shallow breath on aching lungs;
suppress a tickle in my throat,
and feel tears prick to my eyes for a moment,
when your fingers interlaced with mine.

the filtered light captured me,
in a cocoon,
held in suspension high above,
as you brought me into focus;

framed by curled leaves and age-old silken
trapeze lines.
you tilted your head in careful concentration,
opened the aperture wide.
over-exposure washing my face,
and rendered it immaculate.
as Turin, the shroud bore the image,
and yet obscured all scalded scars

when the smoke settles,
draw your camera again,
to see through all anomalies of light and shade,
and capture me.

*//*

# breathe again

//

now, submerge the skin,
rinse grime and meconium,
off to breathe again.

//

# home remedies

//

excerpts from the best-selling "The Complete Encyclopedia of Home Remedies"

"- for irrational fear -

over a low heat, combine one tablespoon of honey, ¼ teaspoon almond flour,
half a cinnamon stick, a tablespoon of fine sugar, six mint leaves and 20g oats. When bubbling, take off the heat and set aside. Slice a fig in halves and poach for four minutes or until the skin begins to peel away. scoop out the fig seeds and add to the rest of the concoction. serve with a spoon.

- for seething anger -

remove the stalks of two mushrooms and the seeds from two squashes, dice and fry on a low heat with oil. add ¼ teaspoon paprika, lime zest from a lime, 20g sesame seeds and 20g pine nuts. once the squash is cooked through, pour in

80ml stock and stir continuously. serve with a
sprig of rosemary.

- for all forms of deep sadness -

take 50ml of milk and a generous teaspoon of
poppy seeds, stirring together over the stove to
simmer for ten minutes. set aside to cool.
use the mortar and pestle to grind 20g
macadamia nuts, a pinch of star anise, 5g
powdered cacao, ¼ dried chili and a pinch of
salt. Once ground, gently combine with the milk
and simmer until reduced. strain and serve
warm, a guaranteed cure.``

//

# herein lies the heart

*//*

herein lies the heart,
formed through entangled silver networks of
veins,
Humors and Virtues;
pliant to its maker's fine design.

exposed to the elements,
the heart begins to calcify;
just as it was never meant to.
silty sediment builds up and petrifies,
raised hackles as a chieftain's armor and title.

leaving only a shell;
to be sanded smooth under rolling tides.
could it be a temporary residence?

*//*

# vegemite

//

vegemite toast,
after the ghost of yesterday,
boasts vitamin A,
and B,
see a rose in every cheek.
a fatigued glow before the week began.

//

# sunburn



sunscreen cast aside in teen exhibitionism,
exposed skin to the elements,
I roll over on my towel,
slip oil over my angled shoulders,
and bask in irresponsibility.
I burn for you,
and turned for you,
I curled the pages of my words for me too.
the silken small of your back,
yearned for,
tell-tale blistered curves ensue.

# the graduate



the graduate sat,
in the back seat of an uber,
silver confetti resting on his shoulders.
I've done it, he thought quietly to himself,
I've done it.
a swift tug on the red cord
loosened the bow.
the scroll sprung open and
he smoothed its creased form
to reveal,
the world.
smaller, for sure - yet there it lay.
in fine, sweeping detail,
just as Prof. E.B. had promised.
but even still,
nothing can fully prepare the graduate.
the blood drained from his face,
shallow, sharp breaths erupted from
trembling lips.
the world as it lay,
curled but now within reach,
made his stomach flip.
he slowly looked out the window,

prying fear's sinister fingers from his heart,
and his side.
the silver fluttered from his robe,
and breathing out,
the graduate opened his gum wrapper,
inscribing,
i am not done, i've begun.

//